Vanna White, America's favorite spokesperson for more than soft premium basic, is the easy care yarn she loves enough to call her own. With its supple hand and stunning stitch quality, Vanna's Choice has the versatility to help you create the designs of your dreams. Make a simple sweater, shape a stylish shawl, or fashion a stunning afghan. With Vanna's Choice, mixing and matching colors has never been easier-or more exciting. The shades in this palette coordinate well together, so you can spend less time second-guessing your color choices and more time getting great results.

About Lion Brand® Yarn Company

Lion Brand Yarn Company is America's oldest hand knitting yarn brand. Founded in 1878, Lion Brand Yarn Company is a leading supplier of quality hand knitting and crochet yarns. Throughout its history, Lion Brand Yarn has been at the forefront of yarn trends while consistently providing its customers with the highest quality product at a value price. The company's mission is to provide ideas, inspiration and education to yarn crafters.

VANNA'S CHOICE® YARNS

Vanna's Choice® Prints and Mists

Mountain Print #200

Woods Print #201

Purple Print #202

Autumn Print #203

Charcoal Print #204

Denim Mist #300

Rose Mist #301

Taupe Mist #302

Purple Mist #303

Seaspray Mist #304

Pearl Mist #305

Tangerine Mist #306

Vanna's Choice®

Linen #099

White #100

Pink #101

Silver Blue #105

Sapphire #107

Dusty Blue #108

Colonial Blue #109

Navy #110

Vanna's Fashions

Scarlet #113	Beige #123	Toffee #124	Taupe #125
Chocolate #126	Espresso #127	Honey #130	Brick #133
Terracotta #134	Rust #135	Dusty Rose #140	Wild Berry #141
Rose #142	Antique Rose #143	Magenta #144	Eggplant #145
Dusty Purple #146	Purple #147	Burgundy #148	Silver Grey #149
Charcoal Grey #151	Black #153	Mustard #158	Pea Green #170
Fern #171	Kelly Green #172	Dusty Green #173	Olive #174
Cranberry #180			

Vanna Choice Yarns

ANNA RIPPLE AFGHAN

EASY

SIZE
42 x 46 in. (106.5 x 117 cm)

MATERIALS
LION BRAND® VANNA'S CHOICE®
> #099 Linen 2 skeins (A)
> #148 Burgundy 2 skeins (B)
> #124 Toffee 2 skeins (C)
> #101 Pink 2 skeins (D)
> or colors of your choice

LION BRAND crochet hook size J-10 (6 mm)
LION BRAND large-eyed blunt needle

GAUGE
11 dc = 4 in. (10 cm).
BE SURE TO CHECK YOUR GAUGE.

STITCH EXPLANATION
Dc2tog (dc decrease) (Yarn over and draw up a lp in next dc, yarn over and draw through 2 lps) twice, yarn over and draw through all 3 lps on hook.

> **TIP**
> The clear plastic zippered bags that many new bed linens are packaged in (sheets, blankets, etc.) make great project bags or yarn storage bags. They are strong, clear, have nice zippers, are "free" and if you use them rather than toss them it's a great way to "recycle"!

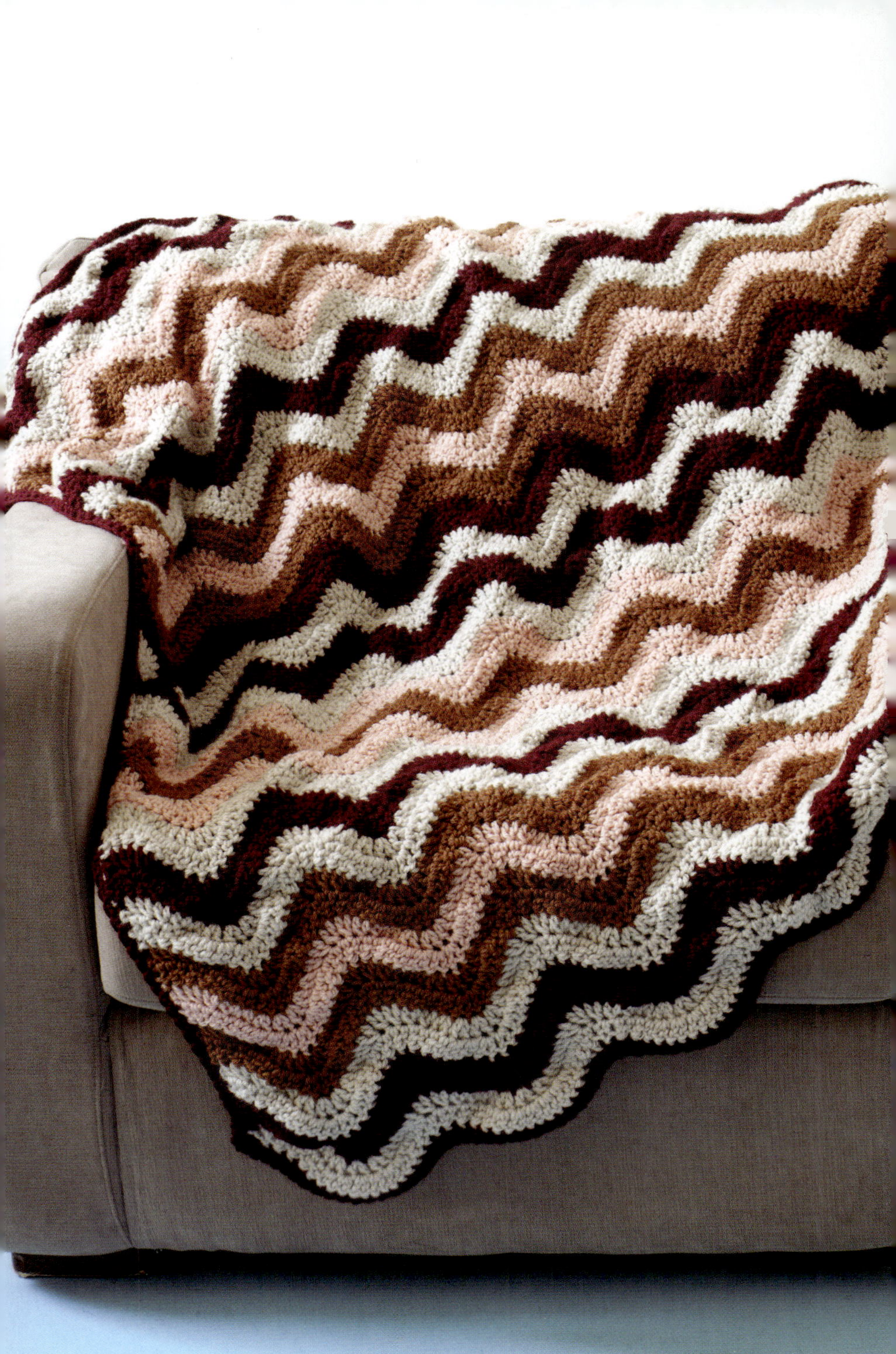

COLOR SEQUENCE
Work 2 rows of each color in the following sequence:
A, B, A, C, D, C, A, B, A, D, C, D, B.

AFGHAN
With A, ch 150.

Row 1 (RS): Dc in 4th ch from hook, dc in next ch, dc2tog 3 times, * 2 dc in each of next 6 ch, dc2tog 6 times; rep from * across to last 8 ch, end with dc2tog 3 times, dc in each of next 2 ch.

Row 2 (WS): Ch 3, turn (ch 3 counts as first dc.) Dc in 2nd dc from hook, dc2tog 3 times,* 2 dc in each of next 6 dc, dc2tog 6 times; rep from * across to last 8 dc, end with dc2tog 3 times, dc in next 2 dc.

Rep Row 2, continuing in color sequence. Work sequence twice. Then work 2 rows each of A, B, and A. Fasten off.

FINISHING
Edging
From RS, join B with sl st along edge of Afghan. Work 2 rounds of sc evenly spaced around Afghan, working 3 sc in each corner. Fasten off. Weave in ends.

CURLY SCARF

Shown on page 9.

Scarf is made in two halves to create symmetrical curls.

EASY

SIZE
About 3 x 72 in. (7.5 x 183 cm)

MATERIALS
LION BRAND® VANNA'S CHOICE®
   #144 Magenta 3 balls
   or color of your choice
LION BRAND crochet hook size I-9 (5.5 mm)
LION BRAND large-eyed blunt needle

ADDITIONAL MATERIALS
3½ in. (9 cm) piece of cardboard

GAUGE
13 dc = 4 in. (10 cm).
EXACT GAUGE IS NOT ESSENTIAL TO THIS PROJECT.

> **TIP** If you are crocheting too tightly, perhaps you are not sliding the work back far enough onto the hook.

SCARF
First Half
Ch 90.

Row 1: Work 2 dc in 3rd ch from hook and in each ch across.

Row 2: Ch 3, turn, dc in same space, 2 dc in each st across.

Row 3: Ch 3, turn, dc in same space, dc in next st, *2 dc in next st, dc in next st; rep from * across.

Row 4: Ch 2 (does not count as st), turn, *hdc in each of next 2 sts, 2 hdc in next st; rep from * across.
Fasten off.

Second Half
Make same as First Half.

FINISHING
Sew halves together so that each half curls away from the center back seam.

Tassels
Wrap yarn around cardboard 40 times. Cut a piece of yarn 10 in. (25.5 cm) long and thread doubled onto large-eyed blunt needle. Insert needle under all strands at upper edge of cardboard. Pull tightly and knot securely. Cut yarn loops at lower edge of cardboard. Tie a Tassel to each end of Scarf. Trim Tassel ends evenly.
Weave in ends.

Curly Scarf | 9

TEA WRAP

INTERMEDIATE

SIZE
18 x 55 in. (45.5 x 139.5 cm)

MATERIALS
LION BRAND® VANNA'S CHOICE®
#140 Dusty Rose 3 balls
or color of your choice
LION BRAND crochet hook size N-13 (9 mm)
LION BRAND large-eyed blunt needle

GAUGE
8 sts + 4 rows = 4 in. (10 cm) in dc.
BE SURE TO CHECK YOUR GAUGE.

STITCH EXPLANATION
Shell Work 5 dc in indicated st.
Half-shell Work 3 dc in indicated st.

WRAP
Ch 3; join with sl st in first ch to form a ring.

Row 1: Ch 3 (does not count as a st), work 9 dc in ring; do not join.

Row 2: Ch 3, turn, shell in first dc, (sk next dc, sc in next dc, sk next dc, shell in next dc) twice – 3 shells.

> **TIP**
> After making a copy of a diagram, I use a highlighter after finishing the row. This shows what I have done and what needs to be done on the next row without covering up the last row.

Tea Wrap | 11

Row 3: Ch 3, turn, shell in first dc, sk next dc, (sc in next dc, sk next 2 dc, shell in next sc, sk next 2 dc) twice, sc in next dc, sk next dc, shell in last dc – 4 shells.

Row 4: Ch 3, turn, half-shell in first dc, sk next dc, sc in next dc, *sk next 2 dc, shell in next sc, sk next 2 dc, sc in next dc; rep from * across to last 2 dc, sk next dc, half-shell in last dc – 3 shells and 2 half-shells.

Row 5: Ch 3, turn, dc in each st across – 25 dc.

Row 6: Ch 3, turn, shell in first dc, *sk next dc, sc in next dc, sk next dc, shell in next dc; rep from * across – 7 shells.

Row 7: Rep Row 4 – 6 shells and 2 half-shells.

Row 8: Ch 1, turn, sc in first dc, *sk next 2 dc, shell in next dc, sk next 2 dc, sc in next dc; rep from * across – 7 shells.

Row 9: Ch 3, turn, shell in first sc, *sk next 2 dc, sc in next dc, sk next 2 dc, shell in next sc; rep from * across – 8 shells.

Rows 10–21: Rep Rows 4–9 twice – 23 shells.

Rows 22 and 23: Rep Rows 4 and 5 – 139 dc. Fasten off.

FINISHING
Edging
From right side, join yarn with sl st anywhere along outside edge of Wrap.

Round 1: Working in sts and ends of rows around all edges of Wrap, work (sc in next st, dc in next 2 sts, tr in next 2 sts, dc in next 2 sts) evenly spaced around. Fasten off.

Weave in ends.

VILLAGE SQUARE AFGHAN

Chart shown on page 25.   *Shown on page 15.*

■■□□ EASY +

SIZE
42 x 42 in. (106.5 x 106.5 cm)

MATERIALS
LION BRAND® VANNA'S CHOICE®
- #099 Linen 2 balls (A)
- #173 Dusty Green 2 balls (B)
- #105 Silver Blue 2 balls (C)
- #135 Rust 2 balls (D)
- #158 Mustard 2 balls (E)
- #133 Brick 2 balls (F)
- or colors of your choice

LION BRAND crochet hook size J-10 (6 mm)
LION BRAND large-eyed blunt needle

GAUGE
Square = 6 in. (15.25 cm).
BE SURE TO CHECK YOUR GAUGE.

> **TIP**
> To keep the size readable on a plastic crochet hook, use a fine tipped permanent marker to write the size right on the end. The mark won't wear off with use, and you won't have to squint to see what size it is.

SQUARE 1
With C, ch 4, sl st in beg ch to form a ring.

Rnd 1: Ch 3 (counts as beg dc), 2 dc in ring, (ch 3, 3 dc in ring) 3 times, ch 3, join with sl st in top of ch-3. Fasten off C. Join D between beg ch-3 of Rnd 1 and next dc.

Rnd 2: Ch 4 (counts as dc, ch 1), dc between next 2 dc, (ch 1, dc) 3 times in next ch-3 sp, * (ch 1, dc between next 2 dc) twice, (ch 1, dc) 3 times in next ch-3 sp, rep from * around, end ch 1, join with sl st in 3rd ch of ch-4. Fasten off D.
Join B in last ch-1 sp made.

Rnd 3: Ch 3 (counts as beg dc), dc in same space, (2 dc in next ch-1 sp) 3 times, * ch 2 – corner made, (2 dc in next ch-1 sp) 5 times, rep from * around, ch 2, work 2 dc in last ch-1 sp, join with sl st in top of ch-3. Fasten off B. Join E between any 2 dc.

Rnd 4: Ch 3 (counts as beg dc), * dc between each dc to corner ch-2 sp, (2 dc, ch 2, 2 dc) in corner, rep from * around, join with sl st in top of ch-3. Fasten off E.
Join A between any 2 dc.

Rnd 5: With A, rep Rnd 4. Fasten off.

Make number of Squares in each color sequence listed below, for a total of 49 Squares.

SQUARE 1: C, D, B, E, A - Make 12 total of Square 1.
SQUARE 2: E, A, D, F, C - Make 13 total of Square 2.
SQUARE 3: F, C, E, D, B - Make 13 total of Square 3.
SQUARE 4: A, D, E, B, F - Make 11 total of Square 4.

FINISHING
Sew Squares together following Assembly Diagram. Weave in ends.

Village Square Afghan

TUMBLING CUBES AFGHAN

INTERMEDIATE

SIZE
44 x 64 in. (112 x 162.5 cm)

MATERIALS
LION BRAND® VANNA'S CHOICE®
- #126 Chocolate 4 balls (A)
- #125 Taupe 1 ball (B)
- #130 Honey 1 ball (C)
- #107 Sapphire 2 balls (D)
- #173 Dusty Green 1 ball (E)
- #143 Antique Rose 2 balls (F)
- #172 Kelly Green 1 ball (G)
- #174 Olive 1 ball (H)
- #170 Pea Green 1 ball (I)
- #144 Magenta 1 ball (J)
- #145 Eggplant 1 ball (K)
- #135 Rust 1 ball (L)
- #108 Dusty Blue 1 ball (M)
- #124 Toffee 1 ball (N)
- #099 Linen 1 ball (O)
- or colors of your choice

LION BRAND large-eyed blunt needle

ADDITIONAL MATERIALS
Circular knitting needle size 8 (5 mm), 40 in. (101.5 cm) long

Tumbling Cubes Afghan | 17

GAUGE
16 sts + 22 rows = 4 in. (10 cm) in St st (k on RS, p on WS).
BE SURE TO CHECK YOUR GAUGE.

NOTES
1. When changing colors, twist yarns on WS to prevent holes.
2. Circular needle is used to accommodate large number of sts. Work back and forth as if working on straight needles.
3. Work Chart from right to left on RS rows, from left to right on WS rows.

AFGHAN
With A, cast on 160 sts.

Chart Row 1 (RS): Working back and forth on circular needle, knit, following Chart Row 1 from right to left and repeating 80 sts of Chart twice.

Chart Row 2 (WS): Purl, following Chart Row 2 from left to right and repeating 80 sts of Chart twice.

Working in St st (k on RS, p on WS) continue chart as established until Row 92 has been completed. Rep Rows 1–92 twice more, then rep Rows 1–46 once more. Do not bind off, but continue with color A for border.

Border
Color Sequence for Border
1 row A, 4 rows D, 2 rows A, 4 rows F, 2 rows D, 4 rows A.

Top Border
With A, k 1 row.
*Work in Garter st (k every row), following Color Sequence and increasing 1 st at beg of every row. When Color Sequence has been completed, bind off.**

Lower Border
With RS facing and A, pick up and k 160 sts across lower edge of Afghan. Rep from * to ** of Top Border.

Side Borders
With RS facing and A, pick up and k 242 sts along one side edge. Rep from * to ** of Top Border. Rep across opposite edge.

FINISHING
Seam mitered corners of Borders. Weave in ends.

Tumbling Cubes Afghan (page 16)

80 sts (rep twice for Afghan)

Tumbling Cubes Afghan (page 16)

- #126 Chocolate (A)
- #125 Taupe (B)
- #130 Honey (C)
- #107 Sapphire (D)
- #173 Dusty Green (E)
- #143 Antique Rose (F)
- #172 Kelly Green (G)
- #174 Olive (H)
- #170 Pea Green (I)
- #144 Magenta (J)
- #145 Eggplant (K)
- #135 Rust (L)
- #108 Dusty Blue (M)
- #124 Toffee (N)
- #099 Linen (O)

TIP

Not having enough yarn for a project is a major concern. Yarn is a multiple purchase item-that means when you purchase yarn, you are generally going to buy several skeins/balls at a time. Many of the projects have multiple colors so it is important for you to purchase enough of each color called for. Visit https://www.lionbrand.com/updates/yarns/yarnchart.htm for a chart that will help you estimate the amounts of yarn required for many popular projects.

PAINT THE TOWN SCARF

EASY +

SIZE
About 5½ x 60 in. (15 x 152.5 cm)

MATERIALS
LION BRAND® VANNA'S CHOICE®
  #113 Scarlet 1 ball
   or color of your choice
LION BRAND crochet hook size K-10.5 (6.5 mm)
LION BRAND large-eyed blunt needle

GAUGE
EXACT GAUGE IS NOT ESSENTIAL FOR THIS PROJECT.

SCARF
Ch 24.

Row 1: 3 dc in 6th ch from hook, *ch 1, sk next 3 ch, 3 dc in next ch; rep from * to last 2 ch, sk next ch, dc in last ch.

Row 2: Ch 3, turn, dc in first st, ch 1, (3 dc in next ch-1 sp, ch 1) 4 times, 2 dc in top of turning ch.

Paint the Town Scarf

Row 3: Ch 3, turn, 3 dc in first ch-1 sp, (ch 1, 3 dc in next ch-1 sp) 4 times, dc in top of turning ch.

Row 4: Ch 1, turn, sc in first st, (ch 5, sc in next ch-1 sp) 4 times, ch 5, sc in top of turning ch.

Row 5: Ch 5, turn, (sc in next ch-5 sp, ch 5) 4 times, sc in next ch-5 sp, ch 2, dc in last st.

Row 6: Ch 1, turn, sc in first st, (ch 5, sc in next ch-5 sp) 5 times.

Row 7: Ch 4, turn, (3 dc in next ch-5 sp, ch 1) 4 times, 3 dc in next ch-5 sp, dc in last st.

Rows 8-11: Rep Rows 2 and 3 twice.

Rows 12-104: Rep Rows 4-11 thirteen times.

Rows 105-109: Rep Rows 4-9.

Row 110: Rep Row 4.
Fasten off.

FINISHING
Edging: Working in free loops along opposite side of foundation ch, join yarn with sc in first ch, (ch 5, sk next 3 ch, sc in next ch) 4 times, ch 5, sc in last ch. Fasten off. Weave in ends.

Village Square Afghan (page 13)

1	3	2	4	1	3	2
2	4	3	1	2	4	3
3	1	2	4	3	1	2
1	3	4	2	1	3	4
4	2	1	3	4	2	1
1	3	2	4	1	3	2
2	4	3	1	2	4	3

KNITTING NEEDLES

UNITED STATES	ENGLISH U.K.	METRIC (mm)
0	13	2
1	12	2.25
2	11	2.75
3	10	3.25
4	9	3.5
5	8	3.75
6	7	4
7	6	4.5
8	5	5
9	4	5.5
10	3	6
10½	2	6.5
11	1	8
13	00	9
15	000	10
17	---	12.75

CROCHET HOOKS

UNITED STATES	METRIC (mm)
B-1	2.25
C-2	2.75
D-3	3.25
E-4	3.5
F-5	3.75
G-6	4
H-8	5
I-9	5.5
J-10	6
K-10½	6.5
N	9
P	10
Q	15

GENERAL INSTRUCTIONS

ABBREVIATIONS
ch = chain
ch-sp = space previously made
cm = centimeters
dc = double crochet
hdc = half double crochet
k = knit
lp = loop(s)
mm = millimeters
p = purl
rep = repeat(s)(ing)
rnd(s) = round(s)
RS = right side
sc = single crochet
sk = skip
sl st = slip stitch
sp(s) = space(s)
st(s) = stitch(es)
tog = together
WS = wrong side
yo = yarn over

* — When you see an asterisk used within a pattern row, the symbol indicates that later you will be told to repeat a portion of the instruction. Most often the instructions will say, repeat from * so many times.

( ) or [ ] — Set off a short number of stitches that are repeated or indicated additional information.

GAUGE

Never underestimate the importance of gauge. Achieving the correct gauge assures that the finished size of your piece matches the finished size given in the pattern.

CHECKING YOUR GAUGE

Work a swatch that is at least 4" (10 cm) square. Use the suggested needle or hook size and the number of stitches given. If your swatch is larger than 4" (10 cm), you need to work it again using a smaller hook; if it is smaller than 4" (10 cm), try it with a larger hook. The same concept applies if you are knitting. If your swatch is larger, work it again with smaller needles. If your swatch is larger, try smaller needles. This might require a swatch or two to get the exact gauge given in the pattern.

METRICS

As a handy reference, keep in mind that 1 ounce = approximately 28 grams and 1" = 2.5 centimeters.

TERMS

continue in this way or as established — Once a pattern is set up (established), the instructions may tell you to continue in the same way.

fasten off — To end your piece, you need to simply pull the yarn through the last loop left on the hook. This keeps the last stitch intact and prevents the work from unraveling.

right side — Refers to the front of the piece.

work even — This is used to indicate an area worked as established without increasing or decreasing.

BASIC CROCHET STITCHES
CHAIN

To work a chain stitch, begin with a slip knot on the hook. Bring the yarn over hook from back to front, catching the yarn with the hook and turning the hook slightly toward you to keep the yarn from slipping off. Draw the yarn through the slip knot (Fig. 1) (first chain st made, abbreviated ch).

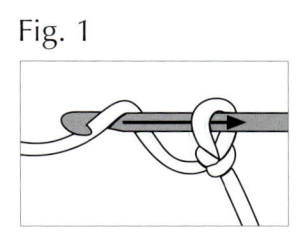

Fig. 1

WORKING INTO THE CHAIN

Method 1: Insert hook into back ridge of each chain (Fig. 2a).

Method 2: Insert hook under top two strands of each chain (Fig. 2b).

Fig. 2a

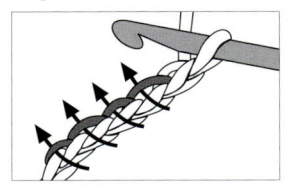

Fig. 2b

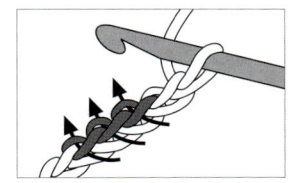

SLIP STITCH
To work a slip stitch, insert hook in stitch indicated, YO and draw through st and through loop on hook (Fig. 3) (slip stitch made, abbreviated slip st).

Fig. 3

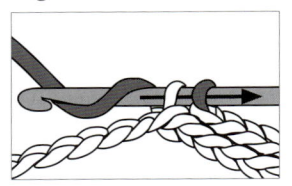

SINGLE CROCHET
Insert hook in stitch indicated, YO and pull up a loop, YO and draw through both loops on hook (Fig. 4) (single crochet made, abbreviated sc).

Fig. 4

HALF DOUBLE CROCHET
YO, insert hook in stitch indicated, YO and pull up a loop, YO and draw through all 3 loops on hook (Fig. 5) (half double crochet made, abbreviated hdc).

Fig. 5

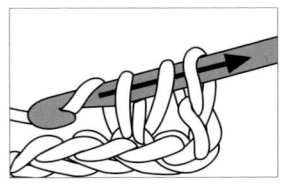

DOUBLE CROCHET

YO, insert hook in stitch indicated, YO and pull up a loop (3 loops on hook), YO and draw through 2 loops on hook (Fig. 6a), YO and draw through remaining 2 loops on hook (Fig. 6b) (double crochet made, abbreviated dc).

Fig. 6a

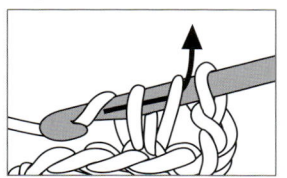

Fig. 6b

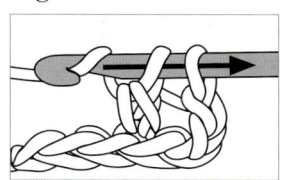

TRIPLE CROCHET

(abbreviated tr)

YO twice, insert hook in stitch indicated, YO and pull up a loop (4 loops on hook) (Fig. 7a), (YO and draw through 2 loops on hook) 3 times (Fig. 7b) (triple crochet made, abbreviated tr).

Fig. 7a

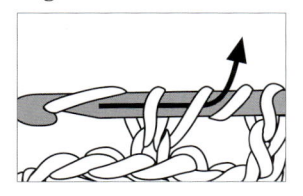

Fig. 7b

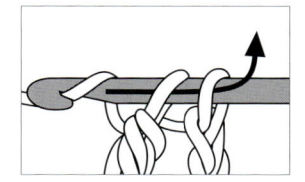

KNIT TERMINOLOGY

UNITED STATES		INTERNATIONAL
gauge	=	tension
bind off	=	cast off
yarn over (YO)	=	yarn forward (yfwd) **or** yarn around needle (yrn)

CROCHET TERMINOLOGY

UNITED STATES		INTERNATIONAL
slip stitch (slip st)	=	single crochet (sc)
single crochet (sc)	=	double crochet (dc)
half double crochet (hdc)	=	half treble crochet (htr)
double crochet (dc)	=	treble crochet (tr)
triple crochet (tr)	=	double treble crochet (dtr)
double triple crochet (dtr)	=	triple treble crochet (ttr)
triple triple crochet (tr tr)	=	quadruple treble crochet (qtr)
skip	=	miss

Yarn Weight Symbol & Names	SUPER FINE 1	FINE 2	LIGHT 3	MEDIUM 4	BULKY 5	SUPER BULKY 6
Type of Yarns in Category	Sock, Fingering Baby	Sport, Baby	DK, Light Worsted	Worsted, Afghan, Aran	Chunky, Craft, Rug	Bulky, Roving
Knit Gauge Ranges in Stockinette St to 4" (10 cm)	27-32 sts	23-26 sts	21-24 sts	16-20 sts	12-15 sts	6-11 sts
Advised Needle Size Range	1-3	3-5	5-7	7-9	9-11	11 and larger
Crochet Gauge Ranges in Single Crochet to 4" (10 cm)	21-32 sts	16-20 sts	12-17 sts	11-14 sts	8-11 sts	5-9 sts
Advised Hook Size Range	B-1 to E-4	E-4 to 7	7 to I-9	I-9 to K-10.5	K-10.5 to M-13	M-13 and larger